I0605995

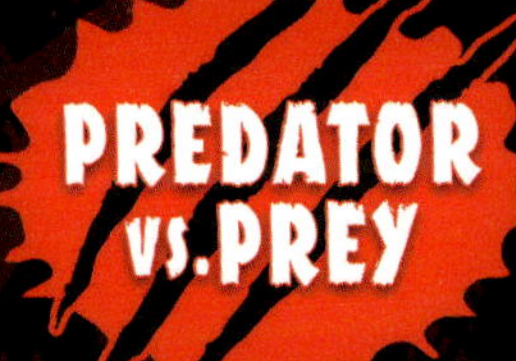

ANACONDAS VS. CAPYBARAS

FOOD CHAIN FIGHTS

BEN HUBBARD

Lerner Publications ◆ Minneapolis

For Jody

Lerner Publications Company
An imprint of Lerner Publishing Group, Inc.
241 First Avenue North
Minneapolis, MN 55401 USA

For reading levels and more information, look up this title at www.lernerbooks.com.

Main body text set in Aptifer Sans LT Pro.
Typeface provided by Linotype AG.

Photo Editor: Lucien Brinkley

Library of Congress Cataloging-in-Publication Data

Names: Hubbard, Ben, 1973– author.
Title: Anacondas vs. capybaras : food chain fights / Ben Hubbard.
Other titles: Anacondas versus capybaras
Description: Minneapolis : Lerner Publications, [2025] | Series: Predator vs. prey | Includes bibliographical references and index. | Audience: Ages 8–11 | Audience: Grades 2–3 | Summary: "Anacondas are one of the world's largest snakes. Capybaras are the biggest rodents and are about the size of a wolf. Discover which animal comes out on top in this battle between predator and prey"— Provided by publisher.
Identifiers: LCCN 2024021229 (print) | LCCN 2024021230 (ebook) | ISBN 9798765647288 (lib. bdg.) | ISBN 9798765662120 (pbk.) | ISBN 9798765656877 (epub)
Subjects: LCSH: Anaconda—Juvenile literature. | Capybara—Juvenile literature. | Anaconda—South America—Juvenile literature. | Capybara—South America—Juvenile literature. | Predation (Biology)—Juvenile literature.
Classification: LCC QL666.O63 H826 2025 (print) | LCC QL666.O63 (ebook) | DDC 599.35/9—dc23/eng/20240613

LC record available at https://lccn.loc.gov/2024021229
LC ebook record available at https://lccn.loc.gov/2024021230

Manufactured in the United States of America
2-1013331-53168-9/30/2025

TABLE OF CONTENTS

CHAPTER 1

DANGER IN THE SWAMP

IT'S EARLY MORNING IN A SOUTH AMERICAN SWAMP. Creatures chirp, chatter, and croak. A capybara stands in the shallow water, eating aquatic plants. But nearby, two eyes rise silently above the surface of the water. A large, green anaconda watches the capybara.

The anaconda has not eaten for weeks and is hungry. The capybara would make a good meal. The anaconda sinks below the surface and swims toward the capybara quickly. But the capybara's herd saw the anaconda. The capybaras bark out warnings. Can they save their herd member? Will the anaconda get its meal?

Green anacondas and capybaras share South America's swamps, marshes, and streams. The anaconda is a strong predator. It speeds through the water. It sneaks up on prey and then strikes! It squeezes prey such as capybaras to death.

But the capybara is not easy to catch. It is large, strong, and built like a barrel. It is a strong swimmer and armed with sharp senses. Capybaras live in a herd for protection. They bark loudly when they see predators. This alerts other members of the herd and helps keep them safe. Let's find out who rules this habitat!

Green anacondas mainly live in the northern parts of South America.

GREEN ANACONDA STATS

WEIGHT: up to 550 pounds (250 kg)

LENGTH: 20 to 30 feet (6.1 to 9.1 m)

SWIMMING SPEED: up to 10 miles (16 km) per hour

CAPYBARA STATS

WEIGHT: 60 to 174 pounds (27 to 79 kg)

LENGTH: 3.2 to 4.6 feet (1 to 1.4 m)

SWIMMING SPEED: 5 miles (8 km) per hour

CHAPTER 2

GREEN ANACONDAS VS. CAPYBARAS

GREEN ANACONDAS AND CAPYBARAS ARE TOUGH FIGHTERS. Both have special skills to help them stay alive. Let's compare their features.

Green anacondas are strong swimmers.

FEMALES RULE!

Female green anacondas are much bigger than males. They are also stronger!

SIZE

Green anacondas are the largest snakes in the world. They are members of the boa family, so they are very heavy. A green anaconda can weigh up to 550 pounds (250 kg)! Anacondas are also long. They can be 30 feet (9.1 m) long. That's about the length of a volleyball net!

Female green anacondas have few predators because of their large size.

Capybaras are about 1.6 feet (0.5 m) tall at their shoulders.

Capybaras are the largest rodents in the world. Most rodents are small mammals, such as mice or rats. A capybara can weigh up to 174 pounds (79 kg). Stretching out to 4.6 feet (1.4 m) long, capybaras are almost as long as a bathtub.

CAPYBARA CHAIRS

Capybaras don't mind small animals and birds sitting on them. They are sometimes called moving chairs.

STRENGTH

Green anacondas have massive, muscular bodies. They wrap their bodies around prey to kill them. The snakes are strong enough to crush a jaguar to death. Anacondas must be tough to survive. They live off the big prey they catch.

FULL FOR WEEKS

An anaconda eats such large meals that it can go for months without food. But then it needs a big meal to fill it up.

A green anaconda wraps itself around an underwater tree branch.

Capybaras have sharp teeth.

Capybaras have stocky bodies and square heads. They have strong jaws and teeth. Their jaws have adapted to bite through sticks and tough plants. Because of their size, capybaras are only hunted by large predators. These include caimans, harpy eagles, and anacondas. Other smaller predators leave capybaras alone.

A green anaconda's coloring helps it stay hidden.

COLORING

Green anacondas have camouflage to perfectly blend in with their environment. Their scaly skin is dark green with blotches of black and pale yellow. Dark stripes appear on their heads. The snake is hard to see among the plants, rocks, and trees. It is even harder to see in the water.

Capybaras' fur is reddish brown and tan. This coloring gives capybaras some camouflage near brown, grassy riverbanks. Their fur is long and thick to keep them warm while swimming. Their fur also dries quickly after getting wet.

SENSES

Green anacondas have excellent senses. They can smell other animals through special chemical sensors on their tongues. They also have pit organs on their lips. These organs can sense the heat given off by other animals. This helps anacondas hunt at night.

Capybaras have a keen sense of smell. They smell water from a mile (1.6 km) away. Capybaras also have powerful hearing. They can pick up sounds that are too quiet for humans to hear. Capybaras communicate with one another by making low sounds.

A capybara pup smells a plant.

SWIMMING

Green anacondas have nostrils and eyes on the top of their heads. This means they can lie almost completely submerged in the water. When they spot prey, they swim underwater to strike. Anacondas can hold their breath for up to fifty minutes. They can also swim at a speedy 10 miles (16 km) per hour. This allows them to ambush prey.

BABY BOOM!

Green anacondas usually give birth to twenty to forty babies. Each one is around 2 feet (0.6 m) long. The baby snakes can immediately swim and hunt.

A green anaconda swims with just its eyes and nostrils above the water.

Swimming helps capybaras keep their skin moist and smooth.

Capybaras spend most of their lives around the water. They are strong swimmers and have webbed feet for paddling fast. Capybaras can swim up to 5 miles (8 km) per hour. Their eyes, noses, and ears are high on their heads. So they can stay almost completely submerged in water.

DIVING DOWN

Capybaras are good divers and can hold their breath for up to five minutes.

AGILITY

Green anacondas are huge. But they are very agile in water. Their smooth skin and strong bodies make them sleek and stealthy. The water helps support their great weight. They can quickly ambush their prey.

A green anaconda swims underwater.

A capybara runs through the water.

Capybaras are agile animals in water and on land. They often enter the water to escape predators and can swim fast with their webbed feet. On land, a capybara can run at a top speed of 22 miles (35 km) per hour.

DUNG EATERS

Capybaras eat their own poop. It might still have nutrients that they missed the first time they ate.

A green anaconda eats its prey.

ATTACK AND DEFENSE STYLES

A green anaconda slithers toward an unsuspecting animal. It strikes with its sharp teeth. Its teeth grip the animal. Then the anaconda wraps its body around the prey and squeezes. Every time the prey breathes in, the snake squeezes harder. After killing its prey, the anaconda opens its flexible jaws and swallows its meal whole.

ROWS OF TEETH

Green anacondas have six rows of sharp teeth to grab prey. But unlike some other snakes, the teeth do not inject venom.

Capybaras are always alert. When they sense danger, they warn those in their herd. Then the capybaras run or swim to safety. Capybaras also have long, sharp teeth to fight with. These teeth can cut through tree bark. So they help as a last form of defense.

SOUNDING OFF

Capybaras make many different sounds, including barks, squeaks, and chuckles. Each sound has a different meaning.

Capybaras can warn one another if a predator is near.

WEAKNESSES

Green anacondas move quickly in the water. But they are slow on land. They are also vulnerable to attacks after eating. This is because their stomachs are so full that it takes all their energy just to digest. They do not move far during this period and cannot move fast.

Green anacondas move slowly on land.

A herd helps keep capybaras safe.

A capybara's best defense is its herd. This gives it safety in numbers. Outside of the herd, capybaras are vulnerable. If alone, their best defense is to run away from danger. They often dive into the water to escape a predator. But being near water all the time has its drawbacks. Many large predators must go to the water to drink.

CATCH A NAP

Capybaras take short naps during the day instead of sleeping longer at night.

CHAPTER 3

RULER OF THE HABITAT

THE ANACONDA SLITHERS TOWARD THE CAPYBARA AT FULL SPEED. It will strike within seconds. But the capybara herd is barking from the shore. The capybara jumps out of the shallow water in fright. It dives into the deep water. It will try to swim away from the snake.

The anaconda is quick. An underwater race for survival begins. Is the capybara faster than the anaconda? The capybara swims at its top speed through the water. But the anaconda doesn't let it escape.

Green anaconda underwater

The anaconda opens its mouth to bite the capybara. The capybara tries to jump away, but it is too slow. The snake bites down hard on the capybara's lower body. The capybara struggles, but it is no use. The anaconda wraps itself around the capybara. There is no escape.

Each time the capybara tries to breathe, the anaconda squeezes tighter. Soon the capybara cannot breathe. The anaconda opens its jaws wide to devour the capybara. Over two hours, the capybara slowly disappears into the snake's stomach. The snake will not need to eat again for months.

Capybaras are just one of many animals anacondas hunt. They also eat wild pigs, deer, birds, turtles, caimans, and jaguars.

Green anacondas are fierce predators.

WHICH ANIMAL WILL WIN?

Today, the green anaconda is the winner of the swamp habitat. But next time, it could be a different story. Perhaps another capybara will escape. The battle of predator and prey continues.

PREDATOR VS. PREY: HEAD-TO-HEAD

ANACONDA

- Massive, muscular body for squeezing prey to death
- Flexible jaw that opens wide to swallow prey whole

CAPYBARA
• Webbed feet for strong swimming
• Teeth that always grow for a superstrong bite

GLOSSARY

agile: able to move quickly and easily

ambush: a surprise attack made from a hiding place

camouflage: colors or markings that help animals blend into their surroundings

habitat: the home of an animal or plant

mammal: a warm-blooded animal that gives birth

organ: part of an animal's body (such as the heart or liver) that performs a certain task

predator: an animal that hunts and kills other animals for food

prey: an animal that is hunted and killed by a predator for food

sense: the ways an animal understands its surroundings. Senses include touch, smell, taste, sight, and hearing.

sleek: smooth or shiny

stealthy: cautious so as not to be seen or heard

LEARN MORE

Adamson, Thomas K. *Anaconda vs. Jaguar.* Minneapolis: Bellwether Media, 2020.

Britannica Kids: Anaconda
https://kids.britannica.com/kids/article/anaconda/352749

Britannica Kids: Capybara
https://kids.britannica.com/kids/article/capybara/634709

Davies, Monika. *Deadly Anacondas.* New York: Gareth Stevens, 2023.

National Geographic: Capybara
https://www.nationalgeographic.com/animals/mammals/facts/cabybara-facts?loggedin=true&rnd=1700851930477

Roggio, Sarah. *Komodo Dragons vs. Wild Boars: Food Chain Fights.* Minneapolis: Lerner Publications, 2025.

INDEX

PHOTO ACKNOWLEDGMENTS

Image credits: Jamie Lamb - elusive-images.co.uk/Getty Images, pp. 4–5; Mark Newman/Getty Images, pp. 6, 24–25; ToniFlap/Getty Images, p. 7 (top); Giedriius/Shutterstock, p. 7 (bottom); Ondrej Prosicky/Alamy, pp. 8–9; FernandoQuevedo/Getty Images, p. 10; Steve Newbold/Getty Images, p. 11; Julian Gunther/Getty Images, p. 12; Jami Tarris/Getty Images, p. 13; © Pete Oxford/Minden Pictures, p. 14; Alejandro MC Photo Collection/Getty Images, p. 15; Nature Picture Library/Alamy, p. 16; Max Fischer/500px/Getty Images, p. 17; WaterFrame/Alamy, p. 18; © Thomas Marent/Minden Pictures, p. 19; gerard lacz/Alamy, p. 20; slowmotiongli/Getty Images, pp. 21, 26; Michael S. Nolan/Alamy, p. 22; elleon/Getty Images, p. 23; Alicia Gonzalez/Alamy, p. 27; reptiles4all/Shutterstock, p. 28; Passakorn Umpornmaha/Shutterstock, p. 29. Design elements: iunewind/Shutterstock; Milano M/Shutterstock; Cassel/Shutterstock; Textures and backgrounds/Shutterstock; Print Net/Shutterstock; Ukrainian studio/Shutterstock.

Cover: Dgwildlife/Getty Images; WaterFrame/Alamy.